Trees

i-SPY

D0784954

INTRODUCTION

Trees are all around us, in parks, gardens, hedgerows, thickets, woods, and forests; and trees are also used to make some roads and streets more pleasant places. Without trees, not only would the world be a bleaker place, it would also be uninhabitable – for trees perform a vital service in removing carbon dioxide from the air and in producing oxygen, the gas that all air-breathing animals depend upon for life. In addition, trees also provide us with many of the foods we eat, such as nuts and fruit, and with products that we use, such as rubber or paper and even, in fossilized form, coal.

The first flowering plants, which include many kinds of trees, did not evolve until about 200 million years ago. Today, despite the widespread destruction of forests – especially tropical rainforests – to clear land for commercial farming and to meet the demand for timber, there are trees all around us. Trees are often beautiful to look at, and many offer food and shelter to a wide variety of animals and even to other plants.

A tree is usually defined as a plant which grows regularly to more than six metres (20ft) in height. i-SPY Trees includes a representative selection of the trees that grow in Britain. Not all of them are native to the British Isles. Some have been introduced for decorative purposes but, in many cases, these have now spread into the wild. We have also included some plants which, often grow as shrubs or bushes but which may reach tree height and that are common enough or interesting enough to be worth describing.

How to use your i-SPY book

The trees and shrubs in the book are listed in two groups. Conifers and related trees are on pages 4–19, with the rest including those that are true flowering plants, from page 20 onwards. In most cases we have tried to show a picture of the full tree and an example of one of its features, such as leaves or fruit, to aid identification. You need 1000 points to send off for your i-SPY certificate (see page 64) but that is not too difficult because there are masses of points in every book. Each entry has a star or circle and points value beside it. The stars represent harder to spot entries. As you make each i-SPY, write your score in the circle or star. There are questions dotted throughout the book that can double your i-SPY score. Check your answers on page 63.

i-SPY Trees is all about getting out and about spotting different species of tree. We have tried to keep our descriptions as clear and simple as possible to help the reader with their identification, there are however a few terms which may need explaining. They are as follows:

Common Name This is the name that most people will use to describe a tree.

Botanical Name This is the Latin name that botanists and other scientists will use to describe a tree.

Evergreen An evergreen tree or shrub is one that keeps its leaves all year round.

Deciduous A deciduous tree or shrub is one that loses its leaves in the colder months of the year.

Origin This is the place where the tree or shrub was first found, even though it may now be found in many places.

Columnar This describes something that is shaped like a column.

Pinnate This describes small leaves when they are arranged on either side of a stalk.

Conical This describes something that is shaped like a cone.

Catkin A catkin is a cluster of little flowers or fruit that looks a little bit like a hairy caterpillar!

Obovate Leaves which are shaped like eggs, with their narrow ends attached to the tree stalk, are described as being obovate.

Palmate Things that are shaped like the palm and fingers of a hand.

Tubular Shaped like a tube.

Crown The top part of a tree or shrub is its crown.

Leader The name for the central or main trunk of a tree.

ATLAS CEDAR

Botanical Name
Cedrus atlantica

Height
Up to 40m

Shape
Pyramid shaped,
with upward-pointing
branches

Leaves Dark or bluish
green needles

Flower, Fruit & Seeds
Pinkish/light brown
cones 5cm to 7cm
long

Bark Dark grey in fine
plates and with deep,
narrow cracks

Evergreen/Deciduous
Evergreen

Origin Atlas
Mountains in Algeria/
Morocco, North Africa

*An Atlas Cedar is
planted on the South
Lawn at the White
House in Washington
D.C.*

INCENSE CEDAR

Botanical Name
Calocedrus decurrens

Height Up to 35m

Shape Columnar

Leaves Dark green, held
together in short sprays
like fans

Flower, Fruit & Seeds
Male flowers yellow,
female greenish before
developing into brown
cones

Bark Flaky, reddish
brown in colour

Evergreen/Deciduous
Evergreen

Origin South-west
United States

Identification Tip Try
looking for its column
shape against the
skyline

*How does this tree
get its name?*

DEODAR CEDAR

Botanical Name
Cedrus deodara

Height Up to 75m

Shape
Pyramid shaped with
drooping branches

Leaves Dark green
needles

Flower, Fruit & Seeds
Upright dark purple
cones

Bark Greyish brown
and cracked into
rectangular plates

Evergreen/Deciduous
Evergreen

Origin Western
Himalayas

Identification Tip The
only cedar whose
leader droops

JAPANESE RED CEDAR

Points: 15

Botanical Name
Cryptomeria japonica

Height Up to 40m

Shape Broadly
columnar

Leaves Feathery
looking, needle-like
foliage

Flower, Fruit & Seeds
Male flowers are
found in clusters at
the tips of the shoots.
The green female
flowers develop into
dark brown cones
with hooks on the
scales

Bark Brown which
peels

Evergreen/Deciduous
Evergreen

Origin Japan

Identification Tip The
foliage is very feathery
and some forms turn
red during winter

*The Japanese call this
tree 'Sugi' and it is
the national tree of
their country*

Botanical Name
Juniperus virginiana

Height Up to 30m

Shape A medium-sized
tree shaped like a wide
cone

Leaves Narrow, bright
green leaves darkening
and shortening to scales

Flower, Fruit & Seeds
Male flowers found
at the leaf tips and
are yellowish. Female
flowers are small and
green. Fruits are egg-
shaped cones

Bark Reddish brown

Evergreen/Deciduous
Evergreen

Origin East and Central
America

*The cones of the tree can
be used to help make
a medicine for treating
kidney disease*

CEDAR OF LEBANON

Points: 15

Botanical Name Cedrus libani

Height Up to 40m

Shape Large wide-spreading tree with very flat arrangement of branches

Leaves Green or greyish green needles in little clusters

Flower, Fruit & Seeds Female cones are 8–10cm long and barrel shaped

Bark Dark greyish brown with short ridges and deep cracks

Evergreen/Deciduous Evergreen

Origin Asia Minor and Syria

The Ancient Egyptians used the resin of this tree to help preserve the bodies of dead people!

Points: 20

PENCIL CEDAR

WHITE CEDAR

Botanical Name
Thuja occidentalis

Height Up to 20m

Shape Medium tree
with horizontal branches
and tips which turn
upwards

Leaves Flattened
scales which are dark
green on top but lighter
underneath

*A tincture made
from Thuja is used
by some people to
try and get rid of
warts and verrucas*

Flower, Fruit & Seeds
Small male flowers are
reddish brown. Female
flowers are greenish or
purplish, developing
into cone-like buds

Bark Orange-brown
with vertical cracks

Evergreen/Deciduous
Evergreen

Origin East and North
America

Botanical Name
Chamaecyparis
lawsoniana

Height Up to 50m

Shape A big columnar
tree with drooping
branches

Leaves Broad sprays of
green scales, shaped
like a fan

Flower, Fruit & Seeds
Male flowers are
reddish when ripe.
Female flowers are
yellowish. Female
flowers develop into
spiky balls, which are
the fruit

Bark Smooth and
brown but can be
cracked

Evergreen/Deciduous
Evergreen

Origin North America

DOUGLAS FIR

Points: 15

Botanical Name
Pseudotsuga
menziesii

Height Up to 100m

Shape Large tree with
conical crown. The
leading shoot is long
with a tuft of shoots
and a slight bend at
the top

Leaves Dark green
above with two white
lines underneath

Flower, Fruit & Seeds
Male flowers are
yellow. Female
flowers are red and
shaped like tassels

Bark Greyish green

Evergreen/Deciduous
Evergreen

Origin North America

*In Canada, bears
scrape off the bark
of this tree so they
can eat the sap
layer underneath*

Points: 15

LAWSON CYPRESS

Points: 15
double with answer

JUNIPER

Botanical Name
Juniperus communis

Height Up to 15m

Shape Conical with
upward-pointing
branches

Leaves Pointed, bluish
green needles

Flower, Fruit & Seeds
Male and female flower
on different trees. Males
are yellow and females
are green. Fruits are
black berries with a
silvery whitish bloom

Bark Reddish brown

Evergreen/Deciduous
Evergreen

Origin Widespread

*What are Juniper
berries often
used for?*

JAPANESE LARCH

Botanical Name
Larix kaempferi

Height Up to 40m

Shape A large tree
with conical crown

Leaves Bluish green
needles held in a rosette

Flower, Fruit & Seeds
Male flowers are round
and yellow. Female
flowers are green and
egg-shaped. Fruits are
cones with scales that
point outwards

Bark Reddish brown

Evergreen/Deciduous
Deciduous

Origin Japan

*These trees do not burn
very easily, and can be
planted in a row to make a
fire barrier*

EUROPEAN LARCH

Botanical Name Larix decidua

Height Up to 50m

Shape Large tree with conical crown. In older trees, the branches droop downwards

Leaves Light green leaves in rosettes

Flower, Fruit & Seeds Flowers are shaped like cones. Male flowers are yellow and female flowers are red. Fruits are egg-shaped cones which point upwards

Bark Greyish brown and falls away in plates

Evergreen/Deciduous Deciduous

Origin European Alps

Capercaillie (a big bird like a grouse) like eating the buds of the European Larch

Points: 20

GUM TREE OR CIDER GUM

Botanical Name
Eucalyptus gunnii

Height Up to 37m

Shape Upright tree
usually grown with
multiple stems

Leaves On
young plants the
leaves are round,
becoming sickle
shaped as it
matures. Leaves
are silver blue

**Flower, Fruit &
Seeds** Small white
flowers in summer

Bark Whitish green
peeling to expose
yellow-grey green

**Evergreen/
Deciduous**
Evergreen

Origin Tasmania

*Eucalyptus oil is used
to help relieve the
symptoms of coughs
and colds*

12

MAIDENHAIR TREE

Botanical Name
Ginkgo biloba

Height Up to 30m

Shape Conical

Leaves Fan shaped

Flower, Fruit & Seeds
Male and female
flowers grow on
separate trees. Male
trees have catkins
whilst female trees
have small fruits in
clusters of three

Bark Brown and
rough

Evergreen/Deciduous
Deciduous

Origin China

Identification Tip
Most plants you come
across are male and
are very upright in
form. Great autumn
colour – the leaves
turn yellow before
falling

*When dinosaurs
roamed the planet,
there were more of
these trees than any
other species*

MONKEY PUZZLE

Botanical Name
Araucaria araucana

Height Up to 30m

Shape Single clear stem with broad conical top

Leaves Bright green, triangular, about 3–4cm across at base

Flower, Fruit & Seeds Male cones grow in clusters. Female cones are round

Bark Dark grey, smooth when young. Dull grey with vertical, smooth wrinkles or cracked into small, rough, round plates

Evergreen/Deciduous Evergreen

Origin Chile

Identification Tip Usually seen on its own

This tree got its funny name because someone once said it would be a very puzzling tree for a monkey to climb!

14

AUSTRIAN OR CORSICAN PINE

Botanical Name
Pinus nigra

Height Up to 40m

Shape An untidy dome. Older trees have upswept branches

Leaves Needles are 8–10cm long and grow in pairs

Flower, Fruit & Seeds
Male flowers are 1–3cm long and grow at the base of small shoots. Female flowers grow at the end of shoots and are dull pink. Cones are 5–8cm long, yellowish brown turning to whitish brown

Bark Dark brown, widely split by flaking cracks

Evergreen/Deciduous
Evergreen

Origin Central-Southern Europe

The favourite tree of Lord of the Rings author J.R.R.Tolkien

Botanical Name
Pinus sylvestris

Height Up to 35m

Shape Either a tall-stemmed or a low-spreading tree

Leaves Bluish green needles which grow in pairs

Flower, Fruit & Seeds Yellow male flowers grow scattered up weak shoots. Female flowers are red and grow on the tips of strong shoots. Cones are egg-shaped and release winged seeds

Bark Grey, turning to scaling pinkish red when young but a dark red when older

Evergreen/Deciduous Evergreen

Origin Spain, Scotland, Northern Europe

As the name suggests, the Scots Pine is the national tree of Scotland!

Botanical Name
Picea abies

Height Up to 60m

Shape Conical

Leaves Small, prickly needles

Flower, Fruit & Seeds Male flowers are yellow. Female flowers are pinkish and develop into cylindrical cones

Bark Pale, reddish brown

Evergreen/Deciduous Evergreen

Origin North and Central Europe

Every year the people of Oslo in Norway send a Norway Spruce to London as a Christmas tree, and it stands in Trafalgar Square

COAST REDWOOD OR CALIFORNIAN REDWOOD

Botanical Name
Sequoia sempervirens

Height Up to 120m

Shape Columnar
with thick trunk and
sweeping branches

Leaves Flattened
needles turning
brown in winter

Flower, Fruit & Seeds
Male flowers are
yellow. Female
flowers are green and
ripen into a round,
brown cone about
2–3cm long

Bark Reddish brown
with soft, spongy or
stringy bark

Evergreen/Deciduous
Evergreen

Origin Western United
States

*How long can a
Coast Redwood
live?*

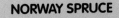

Points: 15

NORWAY SPRUCE

SITKA SPRUCE

Points: 15

Botanical Name
Picea sitchensis

Height Up to 50m

Shape Broadly conical

Leaves Dark green,
sharply-pointed needles

Flower, Fruit & Seeds
Male flowers are yellow.
Female flowers are red
and only grow at the
very top of the tree

Bark Purplish or
greyish brown

Evergreen/Deciduous
Evergreen

Origin North America

YEW

Points: 15

Botanical Name
Taxus baccata

Height Up to 20m

Shape A very broad,
loosely-rounded cone

Leaves Dark green, flat
needles

Flower, Fruit & Seeds
Male flowers are yellow
and produce a lot of
pollen. Female flowers
turn into soft, red berries

Bark Flaking
reddish brown

Evergreen/Deciduous
Evergreen

Origin Europe, Western
Asia, Algeria

*Yews are often planted
in churchyards. The
Cornish believed that
they gave pallbearers
the best protection from
the south-west winds*

WELLINGTONIA OR GIANT SEQUOIA

Botanical Name
Sequoiadendron
giganteum

Height Up to 90m

Shape Conical

Leaves Green scales

Flower, Fruit & Seeds
Male flowers are
whitish yellow and
can be seen until
winter at the tips
of shoots. Female
flowers are green
and then develop as
cones

Bark Dark reddish
brown which is very
stringy. Sometimes it
can look black as if
burnt

Evergreen/Deciduous
Evergreen

Origin Western United
States

*The world's most
massive tree is
in the Sequoia
National Park in
America. What is
it called?*

Botanical Name
Alnus glutinosa

Height Up to 20m

Shape Conical

Leaves Broadly obovate but can almost be round. Dark green on top, pale green underneath. Leaves have fluff between the vein axes

Flower, Fruit & Seeds Male and female flowers grow on the same tree. Male catkins are long. Female catkins are round and grow in clusters

Bark Rough greyish brown

Evergreen/Deciduous Deciduous

Origin Europe

The famous Rialto Bridge in Venice was originally built using alder supports

CRAB APPLE

Botanical Name
Malus sylvestris

Height Up to 10m

Shape Varies, but can be rounded and spreading or tall and thin

Leaves Oval with jagged edge

Flower, Fruit & Seeds Flowers are usually white but can be pink. Fruits are small like miniature apples, but taste bitter

Bark Brown, which can flake when older

Evergreen/Deciduous Deciduous

Origin Europe

The Ancient Celts called this the 'tree of love'. Crab apples can be used to make a jelly, which was traditionally served with meat

APPLE

Botanical Name
Malus domestica

Height Up to 15m

Shape Variable

Leaves Oval with a
jagged edge

Flower, Fruit & Seeds
Flowers white or pink,
fruit very variable

Bark Brown

Evergreen/Deciduous
Deciduous

Origin Europe

Identification Tip This
is the common apple
that we eat so look
out for signs of fruit

China produces more
apple juice than any
other country in the
world at the moment

ASH

Botanical Name
Fraxinus excelsior

Height Up to 40m

Shape Large tree with
domed top

Leaves Pinnate, dark
green

Flower, Fruit & Seeds
Both male and female
flowers are purplish in
colour

Bark Pale greenish grey

Evergreen/Deciduous
Deciduous

Origin Europe

Identification Tip
During the winter the
buds are black

*Ash is very strong and
is often used to make
baseball bats and
hockey sticks as well as
hammers and oars*

BEECH

Botanical Name
Fagus sylvatica

Height Up to 40m

Shape Large tree with
broad, domed crown

Leaves Green, smooth
(almost waxy) with a
slight wave to the edge
of the leaf

Flower, Fruit & Seeds
Male and female
flowers on same tree.
Male in clusters, female
in pairs

Bark Smooth and grey

Evergreen/Deciduous
Deciduous

Origin Europe

Identification Tip The
tree has many forms
with copper or purple
leaves

*Beech wood is
traditionally used to
make chairs. What is
a chairmaker called?*

ASPEN

Botanical Name
Populus tremula

Height Up to 20m

Shape Open conical
crown with upward-
pointing branches

Leaves Dark green
leaves with a toothed
margin held on long
slender stalks

Flower, Fruit & Seeds
Flowers are long with
male and female
flowers on separate

trees. Male flowers
brown whilst female
are green

Bark Greyish green

Evergreen/Deciduous
Deciduous

Origin Europe and
Asia extending to
North Africa

The timber is commonly used for making matches

DOWNY BIRCH

Botanical Name
Betula pubescens

Height Up to 25m

Shape A medium tree with a rounded, oval crown

Leaves Oval with a single row of jagged teeth to the leaf margin

Flower, Fruit & Seeds Wind-pollinated catkins on both male and female flowers. Females are small, upright and yellowish and the males are green turning brownish and hang down

Bark Reddish brown but can turn greyish when old

Evergreen/Deciduous Deciduous

Origin Europe including British Isles

Identification Tip Very similar to the Silver Birch but the shoots and twigs of the Downy Birch have down on them whereas the Silver Birch has warts

Birch bark can be used to make canoes, and birch oil makes excellent shoe polish

24

SILVER BIRCH

Botanical Name
Betula pendula

Height Up to 30m

Shape Very similar to
the Downy Birch but
the branches hang
down more

Leaves Oval but
with a double row of
jagged teeth at the
margin

Flower, Fruit & Seeds
Upright green female
catkins and hanging
yellowish male catkins

Bark As the tree
matures it becomes
the well-known silver
colour, becoming
marked with black

Evergreen/Deciduous
Deciduous

Origin Europe
(including British Isles),
Asia Minor

*Because young branches
are really flexible, they
make great brooms*

Points: 15
double with answer

BLACKTHORN

Botanical Name
Prunus spinosa

Height Up to 6m

Shape Bushy tree or shrub with thorns

Leaves Oval with a pointed tip and toothed edges

Flower, Fruit & Seeds Small white flowers appear around March/April before the plant has leaves. Blue pea-sized fruits called sloes are produced, often with a grey sheen before later turning black

Bark Blackish brown

Evergreen/Deciduous Deciduous

What is the name of the Irish hand weapon traditionally made from a Blackthorn branch?

BIRD CHERRY

Botanical Name
Prunus padus

Height Up to 16m

Shape Roughly oval shaped with upward-pointing branches

Leaves Oval shaped with pointed tip and finely toothed edges

Flower, Fruit & Seeds The whole tree may be covered in spikes of white flowers. Fruits are small blackish cherries

Bark Smooth, dark greyish brown

Evergreen/Deciduous Deciduous

Origin Europe

Identification Tip The flowers smell of almonds and the cherries are very bitter

Parts of this plant contain cyanide, which is a dangerous poison

Points: 20

COMMON BUCKTHORN

Botanical Name
Rhamnus cathartica

Height Up to 9m

Shape Very dense shrub or small tree with spiny branches

Leaves Bright green, oval and toothed

Flower, Fruit & Seeds
Four-petalled with greenish yellow male and female flowers on separate plants. Fruits are black and grow in clusters

Bark Dark brown or almost black, scaly and cracked to show orange

Evergreen/Deciduous
Deciduous

Origin Europe (including Britain)

A dye made from the bark was used to make maps and paper yellow

WILD CHERRY

Botanical Name
Prunus avium

Height Up to 32m

Shape Strong stem
with a conical crown
becoming more
rounded as the tree
gets older

Leaves Spear shaped,
pointed with toothed
edges

Flower, Fruit & Seeds
White flowers with five
petals. Fruits are bright
red cherries which can
be sweet or sour

Bark Reddish brown,
peeling

Evergreen/Deciduous
Deciduous

Origin Europe

These trees have been around for a very long time. Some wild cherry stones were even found in the remains of a Bronze Age village

COMMON HORSE CHESTNUT

Botanical Name
Aesculus hippocastanum

Height Up to 30m

Shape Large tree with spreading, domed crown

Leaves Palmate with five or seven leaflets

Flower, Fruit & Seeds
Stout flower spikes grow in May which are white with a yellow then red centre. Conkers are produced in a spiny shell and are a great children's game

Bark Dark grey or reddish brown

Evergreen/Deciduous
Deciduous

Origin Native to wild border region between Greece and Albania

Identification Tip
During spring look out for big sticky buds at the end of the shoots

Where does the name conker come from?

Botanical Name
Aesculus x carnea

Height Up to 25m

Shape Very similar to
the Common Chestnut
but smaller and more
compact

Leaves Palmate with
smaller dark green
leaflets than Common
Chestnut

Flower, Fruit & Seeds
Rose pink flower clusters
around 20cm long. Fruit
is the famous conker

Bark Brown

Evergreen/Deciduous
Deciduous

Origin Not known, but
possibly Germany

*The plant is used in Bach
(homeopathic) flower remedies
for helping people suffering from
'excessive fear'*

SWEET CHESTNUT

Botanical Name
Castanea sativa

Height Up to 30m

Shape Columnar, with lower branches becoming more spreading when older

Leaves Oval with a strong-toothed edge and parallel veins

Flower, Fruit & Seeds Yellowish green male and female catkins appear around July.

Fruits are chestnuts which are found in groups of two or three in a spiny husk

Bark Brownish grey

Evergreen/ Deciduous Deciduous

Origin Southern Europe, North Africa, Asia Minor

The chestnuts are delicious at Christmas when they are traditionally roasted on the fire

ELDER

Botanical Name
Sambucus nigra

Height Up to 10m

Shape Small tree with
domed crown

Leaves Pinnate, with
5–7 toothed and oval
leaflets

Flower, Fruit & Seeds
Fragrant, flattened
heads of tiny white
flowers are formed in
June. Fruits are masses
of shiny black berries
growing on red stalks

Bark Light greyish
brown, rugged and
cracked

Evergreen/Deciduous
Deciduous

Origin Europe, North
Africa, Western Asia

*Elders often grow
near to badger setts.
True or false?*

Botanical Name
Ulmus procera

Height Up to 40m

Shape Tall and elegant
with a narrow, domed
crown

Leaves Round or oval,
rough to the touch
above with sharply
double-toothed edge

Flower, Fruit & Seeds
Clusters of prominent
red anthers. Fruit is a
winged seed

Bark Dark brown with
deep vertical cracks

Evergreen/Deciduous
Deciduous

Origin Europe

Dutch Elm disease
killed nearly all the
English Elms in the
UK, and now there
are only a few left
around the area of
Brighton in
East Sussex

WYCH OR SCOTS ELM

Botanical Name
Ulmus glabra

Height Up to 40m

Shape Large tree with spreading, domed crown

Leaves On short stalks, the leaf is oval, rough, and coarsely toothed

Flower, Fruit & Seeds Flower similar to English Elm but more purplish. The fruit is a winged seed

Bark Greyish brown

Evergreen/Deciduous Deciduous

Origin Europe, Northern and Western Asia

How does this tree get its name?

Botanical Name
Juglans regia

Height Up to 30m

Shape Large tree with rounded crown

Leaves 3–4 leaflets on each side of a stalk with one large leaf at the tip

Flower, Fruit & Seeds Small male catkins found in leaf axils. Female flowers are found on tips of shoots.

Green fruits that give way to the brown-shelled walnut

Bark Pale grey and furrowed

Evergreen/Deciduous Deciduous

Origin South-eastern Europe, Himalayas and China

Walnut oil was used by painters to thin paint and clean brushes!

HAWTHORN

Botanical Name
Crataegus monogyna

Height Up to 15m

Shape Very variable but may have globe-shaped crown

Leaves Oval in shape with 3–5 lobes and a few teeth at the tips

Flower, Fruit & Seeds The tree is covered in white flowers in May.

Fruits are red haws which grow in autumn

Bark Greyish brown and scaly

Evergreen/Deciduous Deciduous

Origin Britain and Europe

What other names do you know for this tree?

Points: 10

Botanical Name
Corylus avellana

Height Up to 12m

Shape Large shrub or small, many-stemmed tree

Leaves Heart shaped with toothed edges

Flower, Fruit & Seeds
Yellow male catkins in February and small red female flowers. Fruits are 1–4 nuts in clusters

Bark Pale brown

Evergreen/Deciduous
Deciduous

Origin Europe, Western Asia, North Africa

Turkey produces around three quarters of the world's supply of hazelnuts

Botanical Name
Ilex aquifolium

Height Can grow to
25m, but usually 12.5m

Shape Very variable

Leaves Dark green,
wavy, waxy and prickly

Flower, Fruit & Seeds
Small, pinkish white
scented flowers

Bark Silvery grey and
smooth

Evergreen/Deciduous
Evergreen

Origin Western and
Southern Europe,
Northern Africa and
China

*Holly is used as a
Christmas decoration,
and was traditionally
taken indoors in the
hope that the people
in the house would
survive through the
cold winter, like the
holly did*

Botanical Name
Carpinus betulus

Height Up to 25m

Shape A medium-sized tree with a roundish crown. Often used as a hedging plant

Leaves Very similar to Beech but the veins underneath are more pronounced

Flower, Fruit & Seeds Yellow male catkins and small female flowers with red styles. Clusters of nuts, each surrounded by a leaf-like structure

Bark Smooth and dark grey

Evergreen/ Deciduous Deciduous

Origin Europe, Asia Minor

Often used as a pleached hedge which is a bit like a hedge on stilts. A good example is seen at Hidcote Manor in the Cotswolds

LABURNUM

Botanical Name
Laburnum anagyroides

Height Up to 7m

Shape A small, thin tree with irregular ascending branches

Leaves Three oval green leaflets with silky hairs below

Flower, Fruit & Seeds
Clusters of bright yellow pea-like flowers hang down off the tree in May.

Slender fruit pods, 4–8cm long, contain black seeds

Bark Greenish brown and smooth

Evergreen/Deciduous
Deciduous

Origin Europe

The seeds of this plant look like little peas, but be careful, they are very poisonous

LARGE-LEAVED LIME OR LINDEN

Botanical Name
Tilia platyphyllos

Height Up to 35m

Shape Column shaped
with upward-pointing
branches

Leaves Large, heart
shaped, hairy

Flower, Fruit & Seeds
Five-petalled greenish
yellow flowers appear in
June/July. Small clusters
of whitish nuts

Bark Dark grey

Evergreen/Deciduous
Deciduous

Origin Central Europe
to Northern France and
South-west Sweden

Identification Tip The
tree has red buds

*This is the national
tree of both Slovakia
and Slovenia*

BLACK LOCUST

Botanical Name
Robinia pseudoacacia

Height Up to 25m

Shape Medium tree
with round-headed
crown

Leaves Pinnate with
leaflets in pairs.
Leaves oval in shape,
around 2–4cm long
with short spines at
the tips

Flower, Fruit & Seeds
Hanging clusters of
white pea-like flowers
forming long, brown
pods with black seeds

Bark Deeply furrowed,
greyish brown

Evergreen/Deciduous
Deciduous

Origin North America

*Black Locust wood
is great as firewood,
because it hardly
makes any smoke*

FIELD MAPLE

Botanical Name
Acer campestre

Height Up to 26m

Shape Roundish crown
with branches that turn
up at the ends

Leaves Triangular with
five lobes

Flower, Fruit & Seeds
Yellowish green flowers
with clusters of paired,
winged seeds

Bark Greyish brown
with fine, almost
orange-coloured cracks

Evergreen/Deciduous
Deciduous

Origin Europe

*What is the type
of Maple wood
used by furniture
makers called?*

Points: 20

Botanical Name
Magnolia campbellii

Height Up to 30m

Shape A tall tree which is rather elliptic in shape

Leaves Oval leaves which are dark green above, slightly lighter beneath

Origin Eastern Nepal, Sikkim, Bhutan to South-west China

Mississippi in USA is nicknamed the 'Magnolia State' because there are so many magnolias growing there

Flower, Fruit & Seeds Pink flowers up to 30cm across in Feb/March. Fruit is a cylindrical spike with red seeds

Bark Smooth, grey

Evergreen/Deciduous Deciduous

FOXGLOVE TREE OR EMPRESS TREE

Botanical Name
Paulownia tomentosa

Height Up to 12m

Shape Small to medium tree with rounded top

Leaves Green, heart-shaped leaves which can reach 60cm across

Flower, Fruit & Seeds Purple, tubular, foxglove-like flowers are produced before the leaves

Bark Grey-brown

Evergreen/Deciduous Deciduous

Origin China

In China an old tradition was to plant this tree at the birth of a baby girl. When she was ready for marriage the tree was cut down and carved into items for her dowry

Points: 20

JAPANESE MAPLE

Botanical Name
Acer palmatum

Height Up to 15m

Shape Spreading and
bushy

Leaves Each long-
stemmed leaf consists
of 5–7 spear-shaped,
pointed lobes with
jagged edges

Flower, Fruit & Seeds
Clusters of small, dark
purplish red flowers.
Fruit is clusters of paired,
winged seeds

Bark Greyish brown in
older trees

Evergreen/Deciduous
Deciduous

Origin Japan

*These trees are
grown mainly for
their fantastic
autumn colour*

PAPERBARK MAPLE

Points: 20

Botanical Name
Acer griseum

Height Up to 14m

Shape Small, upright tree with dome-shaped crown

Leaves Trifoliate with stunning autumn colours of red and scarlet

Flower, Fruit & Seeds Flowers are clusters of yellow, hanging flowers. Fruits are winged seeds in horseshoe-shaped pairs

Bark Rich reddish brown that peels off in papery strips

Evergreen/Deciduous Deciduous

Origin China

Botanical Name
Morus nigra

Height Up to 10m

Shape Wide spreading with irregular twisting branches

Leaves Large, heart shaped with toothed margin and hairy on both sides

Flower, Fruit & Seeds Catkin-like flowers with females half the length of males. Fruit looks a bit like a blackberry, red turning deep black, really tasty

Bark Light brown, rough and scaly

Evergreen/Deciduous Deciduous

Origin Western Asia

'Here We Go Round the Mulberry Bush' is a very old English nursery rhyme and singing game inspired by the tree

MEDLAR

Botanical Name
Mespilus germanica

Height Up to 6m

Shape Spreading, straggly tree on short trunk

Leaves Spear shaped with fine teeth near tip

Flower, Fruit & Seeds Single white five-petalled flower in May/June. Orange-brown fruits that look a bit like small apples, but have five sepals on top

Bark Greyish brown and cracked into rectangular plates

Evergreen/Deciduous Deciduous

Origin Southeastern Europe

Medlar fruits have been eaten since medieval times and were used to make a tart flavoured with ginger and cinnamon

BLACK MULBERRY

COMMON OAK

Botanical Name
Quercus robur

Height Up to 45m

Shape Large tree with domed crown

Leaves Roughly oblong but the edges of the leaf are divided into 5–7 lobes

Flower, Fruit & Seeds
Female flowers are small and brown. Male flowers are long, yellowish green

catkins. Acorns are the fruit of the oak tree

Bark Dark brown-grey

Evergreen/Deciduous
Deciduous

Origin Europe

The Oak tree is a symbol of strength and is the national tree of many countries, including England and Germany

☆ **Points: 20**

Botanical Name
Quercus ilex

Height Up to 25m

Shape A broad, wide dome

Leaves Glossy, dark green and oval with spiny edges, a bit like a Holly leaf. They become flatter and smoother as they get older

Flower, Fruit & Seeds
Similar to other oaks

Bark Dark greyish brown

Evergreen/Deciduous
Evergreen

Origin Mediterranean

Holm Oaks are popular in truffle forests because the truffles grow really well in amongst the oak roots

SESSILE OAK

Botanical Name
Quercus petraea

Height Up to 40m

Shape Large tree with rounded crown and branches pointing upwards

Leaves Leaves have longer stalks than the Common Oak and have a line of hairs underneath

Flower, Fruit & Seeds
Typical of all oaks. Acorns are the fruit. These have either no stalk or just a very short one

Bark Greyish and finely cracked

Evergreen/Deciduous
Deciduous

Origin Europe

Wine is often matured in barrels made from this type of oak

COMMON GARDEN PEAR

Points: 10

Botanical Name
Pyrus communis

Height Up to 20m

Shape Narrow, open and often leaning

Leaves Oval, or sometimes rounded, glossy green leaves with toothed margin

Flower, Fruit & Seeds
Blossoms in April with white five-petalled flowers. Fruit is a small pear

Bark Dark reddish or greyish brown

Evergreen/Deciduous
Deciduous

Origin Probably Western Asia

There are thousands of varieties of pears, and not all the fruits are pear-shaped!

Botanical Name
Quercus cerris

Evergreen/Deciduous
Deciduous

Height Up to 38m

Origin Southern Europe, Asia Minor

Shape Large tree with straight trunk and domed crown

Possibly the fastest growing oak species in the UK

Leaves Long, oval leaves, coarsely toothed and shallowly lobed

Flower, Fruit & Seeds Flowers as all other oaks. Acorns are held in soft, bristly cups

Bark Greyish and deeply cracked

51

LONDON PLANE

Botanical Name
Platanus x hispanica

Height Up to 35m

Shape A large tree with large dome and twisting branches

Leaves Palmate with 3–5 main lobes

Flower, Fruit & Seeds Both male and female flowers are round. The females are red and the males are yellow. Fruits hang in burred clusters of 2–6

Bark Mottled brown and grey. Peels in flakes to expose yellow-orange beneath

Evergreen/Deciduous Deciduous

Origin Uncertain, probably Spain

First recorded in about 1663, this tree has become synonymous with London as it survives well in air pollution in the city atmosphere

Botanical Name
Populus alba

Height Up to 20m

Shape A large tree which suckers and often goes on to grow stronger on one side

Leaves Variable shape. Some are triangular and toothed, others are more lobed like a maple. Leaves are white underneath

Flower, Fruit & Seeds Male flowers are red catkins, females are yellow-green. Fruit is fluffy and hangs from the catkins

Bark Smooth and greyish green or white with distinctive diamond-shaped marks

Evergreen/Deciduous Deciduous

Origin Europe

The leaf buds of this tree give out a lovely scent in the spring

BLACK POPLAR

Botanical Name
Populus nigra

Height Up to 30m

Shape A large, heavily-branched tree with upward-pointing branches

Leaves Heart shaped

Flower, Fruit & Seeds Male catkins are red and female catkins are greenish. Fruit is a fluffy seed

Bark Greyish brown with cracks

Evergreen/Deciduous
Deciduous

Origin Central and Eastern Europe

This poplar is often seen planted in rows along the roadsides in France and Belgium

WHITE POPLAR

53

Points: 15

Botanical Name
Sorbus aucuparia

Height Up to 20m

Shape An elegant
tree with roughly
conical crown

Leaves Pinnate with
toothed leaflets in
pairs of 11–19

Flower, Fruit & Seeds
Clusters of creamy
white flowers. Bright
red berries in early
autumn

Bark Smooth and
silvery

Evergreen/Deciduous
Deciduous

Origin Europe

*The Rowan grows
at greater altitudes
than any other tree in
Great Britain*

SPINDLE

Points: 15
double with answer

Botanical Name
Euonymus europaeus

Height Up to 6m

Shape Small shrub-
like tree with many
branches

Leaves Green, spear-
shaped leaves

Flower, Fruit & Seeds
Small, yellow flowers
are followed by red,
four-lobed fruits
containing orange
seeds

Bark Greyish green
becoming tinged with
red as the tree gets
older

Evergreen/Deciduous
Deciduous

Origin Europe

*How does this tree
get its name?*

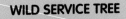

Botanical Name
Sorbus torminalis

Height Up to 20m

Shape Spreading conical or dome

Leaves Glossy green leaves are about 12cm long, deeply toothed with unequal lobes

Flower, Fruit & Seeds Clusters of white flowers

Bark On young trees the bark is smooth and grey, but as it gets older, it becomes flaky and brown, with a pattern like a chess board

Evergreen/Deciduous Deciduous

Origin Europe, Asia Minor, Northern Africa

Because of the 'chequerboard' pattern of the bark, this tree is also known as the 'Chequer Tree'

Points: 25 Top Spot!

Botanical Name
Rhus typhina

Height Up to 8m

Shape Forking branches look like stags' antlers. When the tree is young, the branches are covered in reddish brown hair

Leaves Large pinnate leaves with yellow-orange autumn colour

Flower, Fruit & Seeds
Spikes of yellow male and red female flowers. Clusters of crimson, hairy fruits

Bark Smooth and dark brown

Evergreen/Deciduous
Deciduous

Origin Eastern North America

Native Americans used parts of this tree in their medicines

Botanical Name
Liriodendron tulipifera

Height Up to 50m

Shape Tall, column-shaped tree

Leaves Green, 8–20cm long with four lobes on a long stalk

Flower, Fruit & Seeds
Yellowish-whitish tulip flowers are usually held at its upper reaches. Fruit is brown and bud-like in appearance but filled with winged seeds

Bark Greyish brown

Evergreen/Deciduous
Deciduous

Origin Eastern North America

SYCAMORE

Botanical Name
Acer pseudoplatanus

Origin Southern
Europe

Height Up to 35m

Shape A large tree
with dense crown

Leaves Usually with
five lobes on fruiting
twigs

*Sycamore tree
branches were used
to decorate people's
houses as part of the
May Day celebrations
in Padstow, Cornwall*

Flower, Fruit & Seeds
Hanging greenish
yellow blossoms

Bark Grey and
smooth

Evergreen/Deciduous
Deciduous

Points: 25   **Top Spot!**   **TULIP TREE**

WAYFARING TREE

Botanical Name
Viburnum lantana

Height Up to 6m

Shape Small, bush-like tree

Leaves Oval, minutely toothed with velvety surface

Flower, Fruit & Seeds Clusters of tiny, fragrant creamy white flowers in May/June. Red berries ripen to black in autumn

Bark Brown and hairy

Evergreen/Deciduous
Deciduous

Origin Europe

This tree gets its name because it often grows at the side of the road

Botanical Name
Cordyline australis

Height Up to 15m

Shape Single, clear stem with ascending branches holding the leaves above

Leaves Dense clusters of sword-like green leaves around 40–100cm long

Flower, Fruit & Seeds Flowers are large panicles (branched) of creamy white

Bark Greyish

Evergreen/Deciduous
Evergreen

Origin New Zealand

This is the largest monocotyledon in the world. Maori people made clothes using its leaves

WHITEBEAM

Botanical Name
Sorbus aria

Height Up to 25m

Shape Medium
tree with spreading
branches and dense
crown

Leaves Oval and hairy
beneath

Flower, Fruit & Seeds
Clusters of white
flowers. Berries that
ripen to bright red in
early autumn

Bark Pale brown

Evergreen/Deciduous
Deciduous

Origin Europe

The hard wood was
used for making cogs
for machines before
being replaced by iron

CABBAGE TREE

CRACK WILLOW

Botanical Name
Salix fragilis

Height Up to 25m

Shape A rounded-domed tree on a short trunk

Leaves Long, slender, green leaves up to 9cm long

Flower, Fruit & Seeds
Flowers are catkins, with male and female on separate trees. Fruits are white, fluffy seeds

Bark Greyish with deep cracks and ridges

Evergreen/Deciduous
Deciduous

Origin Europe, Northern Asia

The stems of this tree are very flexible and can be used to make baskets

GOAT WILLOW

Points: 10

Botanical Name
Salix caprea

Height Up to 10m

Shape Shrub with many branches, that can be almost as broad as it is tall

Leaves Oval in shape, hairless on the surface but with fine hairs underneath

Flower, Fruit & Seeds
Flowers are catkins, with male and female on separate trees. Male are yellowish and female greenish. Fruits are seeds

Bark Grey-brown, cracked

Evergreen/Deciduous
Deciduous

Origin Europe (including Britain) and Western and Central Asia

Florists often use the pretty catkins from this tree in bouquets and arrangements

WEEPING WILLOW

Botanical Name
Salix babylonica

Height Up to 20m

Shape A medium tree with round crown and drooping branches

Leaves Long and slender, green above, bluish green below

Flower, Fruit & Seeds Flowers are slender, yellow catkins. Fruits are woolly seeds

Bark Ridged and greyish brown

Evergreen/Deciduous
Deciduous

Origin China

In English folklore, witches use the Weeping Willow as a meeting place as it is said to be enchanted

INDIAN BEAN TREE

Botanical Name
Catalpa bignonioides

Height Up to 15m

Shape A medium tree
with large, rounded
crown

Leaves Green, heart-
shaped leaves are
produced in June

Flower, Fruit & Seeds
Clusters of white
tubular flowers with
an attractive throat
come into blossom in

July or August. Fruits
are long bean pods

Bark Light brown with
deep cracks

Evergreen/Deciduous
Deciduous

Origin Eastern North
America

*This tree is not from
India at all, and takes
its name from its long,
slim pods which stay
on the tree all winter*

INDEX

Answers: P4 Incense Cedar: The wood, resin and leaves are scented.
P10 Juniper: Flavouring gin. **P17** Coast Redwood: 1000 years.
The General Sherman Tree. **P22** Beech: Bodger. **P26** Blackthorn: Shillelagh.
P29 Common Horse Chestnut: Conqueror. **P32** Elder: True. **P34** Wych Elm:
'Wych' is a Saxon word for bendy. **P36** Hawthorn: May, Quickthorn. **P42** Field
Maple: Bird's Eye Maple. **P54** Spindle: The wood was used for making
spinners' spindles.

i-SPY

How to get your
i-SPY certificate
and badge

Let us know when you've become
a Super-spotter with 1000 points
and we'll send you a special
certificate and badge!

HERE'S
WHAT
TO DO!

 Ask an adult to check your score.

Visit www.collins.co.uk/i-SPY to
apply for your certificate. If you
are under the age of 13 you will need
a parent or guardian to do this.

We'll send your certificate via
email and you'll receive a brilliant
badge through the post!